Life After Betrayal:
A Practical Guide

By
Lynda Bevan

THE 10-STEP EMPOWERMENT SERIES

Life After Betrayal: A Practical Guide

Book #2 in the 10-Step Empowerment Series

Copyright © 2007 Lynda Bevan. All Rights Reserved.

First Edition: January 2007

Library of Congress Cataloging-in-Publication Data

Bevan, Lynda.
   Life after betrayal : a practical guide / by Lynda
Bevan.
       p. cm. --   (The 10-step empowerment series ; 2)
   Includes bibliographical references and index.
   ISBN-13: 978-1-932690-31-6 (pbk. : alk. paper)
   ISBN-10: 1-932690-31-X (pbk. : alk. paper)
  1. Betrayal. 2. Man-woman relationships. 3. Adjust-
ment (Psychology) I. Title.
   BJ1500.B47B48 2007
   155.9'3--dc22
                        2006037494

Published by:
Loving Healing Press
5145 Pontiac Trail
Ann Arbor, MI 48105
USA

http://www.LovingHealing.com or
info@LovingHealing.com
Fax +1 734 663 6861

Loving Healing Press

What People Are Saying About:

The 10-Step Empowerment Series

"Through the use of introspective questions the book invites the reader to take a journey of self examination in order to accept the loss and to reengage in life."
— Ian Landry, MA, MSW, Case Manager

"Bevan has real-life experience in the area of loss and 'rebuilding' her life and self-esteem in the face of traumatic experiences such as being abandoned by a partner."
— Margaret M. Mustelier, Psy.D.

"Nowadays there are too many books about adult loving relationships, but they usually are generic and abstract descriptions. This book is different because it moves to specificity and provides concrete steps to overcome a disrupting episode in our lives."
— Carlos J. Sanchez, MA, Family Therapist

"Lynda Bevan delivers what she promises in the title of the book: it is a practical guide and a no-nonsense approach. Her descriptions of the experiences are palpable."
— Chin Tao, LMFT

"This is a well thought out, useful little book that is an excellent guide for those recovering from a broken long-term relationship." — Robert Rich, MSc, PhD, M.A.P.S.,

"The book is studded with illuminating case studies and provides an excellent exposition of issues such as post-traumatic emotional responses, pre-trauma expectations, setting boundaries, forgiveness and acceptance, and the do's and don'ts of moving forward. A gem."
Sam Vaknin, author *Malignant Self Love: Narcissism Revisited*

Table of Contents

Introduction

This book is written for those who have suffered the hurt, humiliation and embarrassment of being betrayed by their partner having an affair.

A relationship is based on trust. When a betrayal occurs trust is destroyed. Betrayal hits the very core of your being, leaving you empty, bewildered, ashamed, and unable to equate or comprehend the situation you are embroiled in.

When you discover that betrayal has occurred, it both rocks your soul and leaves you to question every aspect of who and what you are.

Here are some typical thoughts and feelings during this time:

- I am no longer safe and secure in my relationship.
- I am no longer part of a couple.
- I am no longer able to trust the person I love.
- I can no longer trust myself!

Some questions you may ask are:

- Why didn't I see it coming?'
- Why am I so trusting of my partner?
- What have I done to deserve this to happen?
- What can I do about it?

In the beginning, your mind spins out of control and you become emotionally disabled temporarily.

In this book, I will guide you through the devastating emotions that you encounter by the betrayal of a spouse/partner. It is not an easy ride, but a necessary one if you have both decided to give your relationship a second chance. You will encounter the hard facts of betrayal through each step on the path to intimacy and emotional recovery.

Step 1 Discovering Betrayal

Betrayals come in different guises: they are varied but with some common features. Below is a general list of the different types of behavior of betrayal. I will give you a short explanation of each type of betrayal before focusing on the main purpose of this book: 'betrayal between partner/spouse'.

Different types of betrayal occur whenever:

- A partner has an affair behind your back
- People lie to you
- Someone cheats or robs you of money, property, etc
- People gossip behind your back and you overhear the lies that they are saying
- A parent hurts their child.
- You are let down by someone you trusted, e.g. parent, friend, boss, spouse, child, or sibling
- You are humiliated and put down by someone
- A parent lets you down
- You are betrayed by your own body (as when a serious illness occurs)
- You are betrayed by society

When you are betrayed by your partner

When this happens, the emotions you experience can be extreme. If and when this happens, you must not accept the entire blame or think that the reason this has happened is 'your fault.' Nor does it mean that you are unworthy and unable to sustain a healthy relationship. It says more about your partner's inability to be loyal and honest in their own thoughts and actions. Inevitably, you will question your intuition and perception in failing to detect that your relationship was heading toward a rocky path. You question your own attractiveness and even the intimacy you both shared. In short, you feel a fool.

If your partner has strayed and you are struggling with this feeling, you may experience the following emotions:

• Shock	• Panic
• Disbelief	• Sadness
• Numbness	• Anxiety
• Denial	• Tiredness
• Anger	• Depression
• Hurt	• Loss of confidence
• Unhappiness	• Worthlessness

The above list is similar to that of the grieving process you experience when someone dies.

Here is an example of this type of betrayal:

A gentleman had been referred to me by his General Practitioner as suffering from depression and he had been prescribed anti-depressants. He had been affected for some considerable time. His depression was linked to a substantial loss of finances, when his 'established' business had hit trouble and been liquidated. During our sessions together, he confided that his wife was a professional business woman with an active social life. During their marriage he had always accompanied her to social events. Now, however, she didn't want him to attend any social event with her because she felt embarrassed that his business had failed. He also told me that his wife had no patience with him and was physically and emotionally unsupportive. In fact he said he felt 'in the way'.

I asked him if it would be helpful if I spoke with his wife to explain about depression and the way to overcome it. He readily agreed. I met his wife and she made it plain that she could not understand why her husband was reacting to this situation so badly. She confirmed that she had no patience with him over this issue. She led a very busy professional, domestic and social life and was finding her husband an encumbrance. She told me that she was having an affair which had been established some time before her husband's business had disintegrated as there had been no sexual intimacy between her and her husband for some considerable time.'

To be cheated on is bad enough, but to cheat when your partner is experiencing major financial loss and a traumatic emotional re-adjustment is a double-betrayal.

When people lie to you

In general, people are rarely completely honest in relationships: it's the law of survival. You only get told what the other person wants you to know. Details, (hidden agendas) etc., remain undisclosed most of the time.

Knowing this will help you to understand the games people play in relationships. The dishonesty needn't be detrimental to your relationship. Sometimes incompleteness is used to short-cut an explanation or to dissolve an argument, i.e.

Here is an example: An innocent question: What time did you get home from work tonight?

Answer from an **innocent** partner: About 5.30 p.m.

You might omit the fact that you stopped in at the super-market on your way home because this information is of no interest to your partner. Does that make you a liar?

If, however, you have something significant to hide, the same question answered could have consequences, i.e.

Here is the same example with a difference:

An innocent question: What time did you get home from work tonight?

An answer from a **guilty** person: About 5.30 p.m.

It's the same question and answer scenario but this guilty partner is hiding something, i.e. the guilty partner deliber-ately avoids telling the truth, that s/he went out for coffee with an old flame.

Concealing the truth means you are being secretive in keeping that information from your partner. This indicates that you knew that meeting up with an old flame would be unacceptable to your partner. It also indicates that you might be tempted to repeat the situation.

When someone cheats or robs you

The dictionary explanation of cheating is: an act of decep-tion. An act of fraud, imposture or imposition.

Cheating characteristically creates an unfair advantage over someone, often at the expense of others. There is nothing worse than someone cheating, duping, or robbing you.

Most people would agree that they would rather give something away willingly than be cheated by someone who is prepared to get what they want by any means. Here is an Example:

An acquaintance I knew sent away for a set of CDs on the subject of enlightenment. Upon receiving the CDs he decided that, whilst they were excellent value for money, he would rather copy them and send the originals back. This meant not paying for them and cheating the sender. I thought that example to be highly ironic as the CDs explained how to attain a higher level of consciousness. What a Cheat!

When people gossip behind your back:

You expect those whom you trust to be loyal in word and deed. That trust is immediately broken if that person passes on to another person the stuff you have told them in confidence. We all have secrets; some secrets are larger than others. The last thing we want is for those confidences to be passed on to another person without our consent.

Here are some examples:

- If you meet someone for coffee and your partner finds out from another person (an innocent encounter with a friend/colleague can turn into a nasty situation, if wrongly portrayed)

- If someone makes up stories to put you in a bad light

- If someone deliberately tells lies in order to put you down and elevate themselves

- If someone repeats something you have said and adds more to the story

- If someone sabotages your ideas and uses those ideas for themselves

- If you purchase an item of clothing that was costly and you told your partner that it was reduced in a sale. You tell a friend the true cost of the garment and your friend slips up and tells your partner the true cost of the item you purchased.

> "A rogue gives a ready ear to mischievous talk, and a liar listens to slander." (Proverbs 17:4 NEB)

When a parent hurts their child

Children give unconditional love. **Unconditional love is, loving without conditions limitations or reservations.** In other words, it is love that is undiminished regardless of what the other person does.

Children are innocent and have not yet learned the ways of the world. They have no expectations. They just are. They look to those people who care for them with total trust. If this trust is abused, then their self-esteem lowers and self-worth is destroyed.

In order to raise a child's self-esteem, you must nurture, support, encourage and praise all their efforts. It is the responsibility of parents to look after them and guide their passage to adulthood. However, if this nurturing is negative, then the child will be unable to place any value on who they are and what they achieve in their life.

When you are let down by someone you trusted: intuition

All of us have experienced a situation in which we have found ourselves not trusting another person. Sometimes there is no logical reason for this: it's just a feeling, intuition, gut reaction. Often we are unable to articulate the feeling. In my opinion first impressions are important and shouldn't be taken lightly. The phrases such as, 'I wouldn't trust you as far as I could throw you,' leap out in these circumstances.

Intuition is a valuable tool which can lead you to the core of a problem. Intuition is within you, you feel it in the pit of your stomach. You can learn to recognize and develop your intuition by listening to your inner voice. With practice, you can easily recognize your intuition and make it a valuable tool in relationships.

What does not trusting someone mean?

- It means you are confused regarding the other's issues and motives
- It means you have no confidence in someone's ability to information secure
- It will affect how you will react to this person
- It stops you being spontaneous
- It will erode your relationship with that person

You will be unable to grow and develop with that person. If you have had 'trust issues' previously, you will be even more wary. You will be looking for double meanings and hidden agendas during conversations. Because trust is an essential element in relationships, the relationship will lack quality and substance.

When you feel humiliated by someone

According to Wikipedia, "Humiliation is literally the act of being made humble, or reduced in standing or prestige. However, the term has much in common with the emotion of shame. Humiliation is not in general a pleasant experience as it reduces the ego."

Here are some examples of the effect of being humiliated:

- It lowers your self-esteem
- It reduces the pride you have in yourself
- It makes you feel inferior
- It makes you feel helpless
- It knocks your ego
- It makes you feel bullied
- It makes you feel intimidated

- It can have a lasting effect on your psyche

When a parent lets you down: Patterns of behavior

Your patterns of thought and behavior are established during childhood. You adopt these patterns by copying the behavior of those people closest to you (role models). If, however, you experienced the following in your own childhood:

- If you were neglected (physically and emotionally)
- If you were ignored
- If you were isolated
- If you never had praise
- If you were abused physically
- It you were abused emotionally
- If you were abused sexually
- If you were lied to
- If you experienced domestic violence

…then these difficulties you have experienced and absorbed have formed the foundation for your thought and behavior patterns, which will negatively affect your behavior and self-esteem in adulthood.

When you are betrayed by your body

We live in a culture that promotes youth and physical fitness. Your body image and physical appearance are important to you, and it does affect the way you are perceived by others. Here are some examples of emotions you may feel when your body becomes misshapen, older, diseased, or infected?

- Embarrassed (spots, eye bags, hair loss)
- Shameful (unwanted hair)
- Disappointed (skin sagging)
- Tearful

- Unhappy
- Angry
- Hostile
- Frightened
- Worried
- Frustrated
- Unclean

These are only some of the emotions you experience when you feel your body has let you down. This is especially so if you have always taken pride in and looked after yourself, eaten healthily, exercised regularly, looked after your skin, etc.

It is quite normal to have some of these feelings about yourself and your body after being diagnosed as suffering from a serious illness.

On a more positive note, if you are, or have, experienced physical problems and/or a serious illness you can also feel:

- Proud of the way your body has coped with the illness
- Grateful for your body's resilience and stamina

When you are making the most of your good attributes and viewing yourself positively you will benefit.

Betrayed by Society

You may feel that society has let you down. This can happen if you are:

- Unemployed
- Lack appropriate education
- Isolated
- Fighting for government benefits in order to survive
- Worried about health-care
- In a minority group

- Marginalized by an unpopular, unacceptable illness (HIV+)

Everyone should have the opportunity of gaining suitable education and employment. If these two things are denied, you then feel betrayed by society. Or perhaps you may have experienced a long wait for an appointment to be admitted into hospital.

It is important that you feel cared for and valued as a human being. It is the very essence of being accepted and approved by others that forms part of the quality of your life. If this is not provided by outside forces (society), then you should take action and develop a way of obtaining self-esteem by other methods.

Step 2   Who is to Blame for the Betrayal?

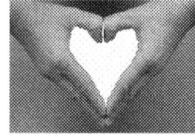

The short answer is both partners! I know that some of you reading this will balk at this statement. However, it is important to clearly assess your relationship up to the point of the betrayal and take responsibility (we will discuss 'responsibility' in detail in Step #7) for your part in the approach of this devastating experience.

You must understand and accept that whatever happens in a relationship you are partly responsible for it occurring. This is a crucial consideration in the 'moving on from betrayal' process because when you have discovered and examined your role in the process you can learn to correct it. If you can't understand or see your part in the betrayal scenario, then you are not looking hard enough at the part you have played. I am not suggesting that you are totally to blame for your partner's betrayal. My point is rather that it takes two people (one acting and the other one reacting) to bring about the situation of betrayal in a relationship.

What is blame?

To blame is to find fault with and hold someone else responsible for whatever occurs in your life.

- Blaming someone disempowers both the blamer and the blamed.
- Blaming someone else is a powerful control tool
- Blaming someone makes that partner feel guilty and frees the blamer from responsibility

If you are the person who is blaming your partner for the betrayal, then you are absolving yourself and not taking responsibility for your part in your relationship with your partner. Also when you blame someone else, you are giving away your personal power and control to them. You must focus and identify your part in the betrayal situation. In seeing your part of the betrayal process you will be better placed to change that part in your relationship in the future.

If you are the person who is blamed for a betrayal and you accept this fact, then you will start to feel remorseful and guilty. This betrayal might have occurred for many reasons. However, as the betrayer in the relationship you must accept that you are the partner who is responsible.

The overwhelming feeling that comes with blame is powerlessness. The **'blamed'** partner must take responsibility for the betrayal that has taken place. The partner who is the **'blamer'** must take responsibility for their part in the process that led to the betrayal occurring. This scenario can trap both partners in a locked situation with no escape. This is a lose/lose situation with both partners experiencing inner conflict and distress. Taking responsibility for our mistakes is vital to personal development and growth and particularly so when in the 'moving on after betrayal' process.

The Blamer

If you are the 'blamer' you are placing the control and responsibility of personal communication, interaction and situations, outside yourself (on to your partner in this instance), believing that you are vulnerable, innocent and powerless in controlling your life because of what other people are doing to you, i.e., your partner cheating on you. You are placing yourself in the 'victim' category.

The partner who is the 'victim and blamer' may believe that:

- Their life is full of injustices
- They have no power of their own life
- They are unable to exercise control of their life
- They are innocent, weak bystanders
- They have limited choices
- They have limited freedom
- They believe that everything they do is wrong
- They believe that everyone finds fault in them
- They believe that they are not good enough and that's the reason bad things happen to them

In order to change your thinking patterns, (see Step #5) it would be helpful if you identified the triggers, conversations, situations and conflict that placed you in the 'victim' category. 'Victims' attract 'victims' to them like magnets ('birds of a feather flock together'). Take some time with this thought and look at the people around you who you can identify as a 'victim.' Can you see, and acknowledge, that they have similar traits to you?

Ask yourself:

- What benefits do I derive from staying in this role?
- Who or what am I afraid of?
- How can I change? (The answer to the question 'how can I change? will be addressed later on in this step).

The Blamed (Betrayer)

If you are the 'blamed' partner who regrets your betrayal and wants to mend your existing relationship, you will feel regret, shame, and disappointment in yourself. You might feel frustrated and angry that your partner is "opting out" of taking responsibility for their part in the lead up to the be-

trayal that has occurred. You are weighed down with the total responsibility and accountability of the betrayal. You will
question your own interpretation of events as you become
convinced by your partner that you are entirely to blame.

The partner who is blamed may feel:

- They cannot do anything right for their partner
- They are an easy target for their partner to put pres-
  sure on
- They feel guilty (because they have cheated on their
  partner)
- They feel guilty sometimes even when they have done
  nothing wrong
- They feel totally responsible for the relationship prob-
  lem
- They feel they are being punished by their partner
- They feel frustrated by their partner's interpretation of
  events
- They feel powerless to change their partner

These examples are just some of the reactions that can occur between two people.

Where does 'blame' come from?

Blame emanates from situations you have experienced in
your early childhood. A child copies the communication
skills, (interactions and re-actions) of their role-models: parents, siblings, grand-parents, aunts, uncles, and friends. Here
are two simple examples:

- If you have seen your mom using blame to control your
  dad, you will store the memory of this situation and will
  use it when you are in a similar situation in the future.

- If you were continually 'blamed' by your parents (or others) during your childhood, as an adult you will, unconsciously, link to the memory of the blamed child you once were and use the same old bad pattern that you know so well that has been stored in your memory box.

Patterns of behavior, are deeply rooted in your memory box, and can affect every area of your life. Blame isn't something you are born with. It is a learned behavior that can be corrected.

We only really learn what our bad thinking patterns are when we become adults. This becomes clear to us when we recognize that we are continually using the same strategies and communication skills that we have used all our lives that have resulted in a negative or blocked outcome. Bad thinking patterns become transparent when we realize that the things we have said have had no satisfactory long-term conclusions. We are going around and around in the same circle with no visible means of escape. Take some time to look back at your relationships and see if you can identify the repeating bad pattern that locks you in.

Blame and Self-Esteem

Blame is linked to self-esteem as the 'blamer' is unable to accept responsibility for who they are and are unable to make any decisions in their life. One of the reasons for this is lack of confidence to stand by what they say or do. It is so easy to blame a partner for their bad habits, faults and the ultimate betrayal of having an affair with someone, and not see your own bad habits and faults. There is nothing you can do to change your partner's flaws; this is out of your control. Only your partner can change their behavior. You can only change your own repeating bad patterns and flaws.

> "The period of greatest gain in knowledge and experience is the most difficult period in one's life."
> —Dalai Lama

Self-Esteem

The self-esteem, self-confidence and self-worth that should be naturally yours are temporarily depleted during times of betrayal. It is hard to value and love yourself when someone has betrayed you. The person who has betrayed you has devalued you in the most intimate and personal way.

Self-esteem is an essential ingredient in any healthy relationship. If you respect and like yourself, you will feel confident and able to interact with your peers. Without self-esteem, you will wither away and emotionally disable yourself. Self-esteem is a fragile set of beliefs. At the 'drop of a hat' it can vanish into thin air. Self-esteem begins in childhood.

Childhood

During your childhood, the emotional, physical nurturing and learned behavior that you experience is absorbed. This establishes patterns that are automatically stored in your memory box (i.e. your mind). These patterns are the blueprint of thoughts, speech and behavior that you will automatically link to and repeat throughout your life. When a child grows up with people who are emotionally aware, the experiences which are passed on to the child are healthy and nourishing. When a child is brought up by people who are emotionally unaware, the experiences passed on to the child are unhealthy and uncaring.

Good Self-Esteem

For many people, it takes years to achieve good self-esteem. It should be allowed to build up within you and can be obtained as a result of achieving some measure of personal fulfillment and success. This personal success gives you a feel-good factor which, in turn, makes you proud of your achievement however small that achievement might be. Even though it may take time for you to develop good self-esteem, it can be demolished in a blink of an eye if it is undermined. Self esteem should be nurtured and allowed to continue developing. A general example of low self-esteem:

A man told me that he felt guilty because he had come to realize that he had been intimidating his partner for some time. This had become apparent to him when he noticed that she was unable to answer the telephone in case she said the *wrong thing*. When forced to answer the phone, she would stutter and hand the phone over to anyone rather than continue with the conversation. He had also noticed that she took their eldest child with her when doing the weekly food shopping. His realization that this was his doing had come about when a work colleague was brave enough to confront him at work, telling him to stop controlling, manipulating and intimidating him. This confrontation with his colleague forced him to think how he was being perceived by others and he recognized that he was a bully and behaving in this way with everyone. He felt very bad about what he had done and asked what he could do to change his ways and be more supportive and encouraging of his wife.

Here is an example of a form of betrayal between a married couple:

A woman once told me that during an argument with her husband, he marched her over to the mirror hanging on the wall in their living room and said, "What do you see in the mirror?' she replied, 'I see you and me'. He looked at her and said, "Well, I see someone who is old, fat, ugly and sexless." His wife was dumbstruck and unable to retaliate.'

Step 3 — Going Back to The Beginning

If one partner in a relationship has betrayed the other, and both partners decide to re-establish a satisfactory relationship, it will be necessary to question the fundamentals of your emotional contract with each other. In order to do this, you will both need to take a journey back to the beginning of your relationship to examine and understand every your basic beliefs of each other. This emotional journey will give you both the opportunity to reassess and reestablish your way of relating and reacting to your partner, and will enable you both to rebuild your future on a solid foundation.

Everyone begins a relationship with hopes, plans and dreams for their future life together. This is part of a normal, loving relationship for people starting their journey through life as a couple. You will probably remember the feeling of being elated, fulfilled and ecstatic in this first stage of your loving relationship. In order to move on from a betrayal, you will both need to examine your true feelings for each other. Starting at the beginning you will need to understand how each of you views the emotion 'love'. Let's examine 'Love'.

What is Love?

During my childhood, true love was epitomized by Doris Day and Rock Hudson. She was beautiful, he was handsome, and they both lived in a fabulous house with roses around the door and had two well-behaved children. How misguided was I?

For the generations that came after me, Prince Charles and Princess Diana depicted the ideal loving relationship. Indeed, the generation that followed these two role models has similar role models by associating love with Jennifer Anniston and Brad Pitt. None of these three examples are actually positive role models for couples establishing or re-establishing a relationship.

Dictionary definition of Love: 'Love is a strong liking for someone. It's a strong affection for another person.'

According to the *Bible* (I Corinthians 13:4-6.)**:**

- Love is patient and kind
- Love is not arrogant or rude
- Love does not insist on its own way
- Love is not irritable or resentful
- Love does not rejoice at wrong
- Love rejoices in right
- Love bears all things
- Love believes all things
- Love hopes all things
- Love endures all things

Love is a powerful force that captures you and holds you for ransom. You will do anything for the person you have 'fallen in love' with. You believe that 'love conquers all.' Falling in love is temporary insanity. Your every thought is eroded, thinking about this person. You think about them 24/7. You feel you have met the person of your dreams and are fulfilling the fantasy of the mental picture you had created. Love is emotionally draining and stops you engaging fully in anything else. You will only see and hear what you want to, and will ignore anything that is in any way detrimental to the relationship. Do you remember this stage of your relationship, when you only saw your partner's good side and were ignorant of the possibility that hidden agendas and unconscious manipulations could occur at a later date?

> "'Tis' better to have loved and lost than never to have loved at all." —Tennyson (*In Memoriam*: 27, 1850)

There are different types of love, i.e.:

- Unconditional love
- Conditional Love
- Sexual Love
- Romantic Love
- Affectionate Love
- Platonic love
- Passionate Love
- Puppy Love
- Infatuating Love
- Committed Love
- Professional Helper & Client

Unconditional Love

...is a love forever. It's all encompassing. It is a desire to share everything you are and everything you have with that one special person. Opinion varies greatly regarding unconditional love. Much is written about loving someone unconditionally.

> Love is not love which alters when it alteration finds. —Shakespeare (Sonnet 116)

My own belief is that unconditional love only exists:

- From God to us
- From baby/toddler to parent/caregiver
- From animal to keeper.

Loving someone 'unconditionally' means that you will never expect them to be a 'peace-at-any-price-person.' All other love is conditional.

Conditional love says that I will love you if:

- You are good to me
- You are patient
- You are understanding
- You are employed

- You are generous
- You are capable
- You will respect me
- You will join forces with me for our future together
- You do not hurt me (physically or emotionally)
- You will like my family.

The list is endless. I believe that most of us love each other 'conditionally'. Loving someone 'conditionally' is having the need to **control** that person. **Control, manipulation and power** are the same side of the emotional coin.

You can control and have power over someone in many ways:

- By intimidatin
- By interrogating
- By physical violence
- By bullying
- By frightening
- By the power of suggestion
- By mind control (games people play to get their own way)
- By false promises
- By manipulation
- By bribing/buying
- By being helpless and inviting care

Ask yourself these questions:

- Whom do you love conditionally?
- Whom do you love unconditionally?

Be honest with your answer. Make a list. Write down the reasons you love each person in the way you identify either conditionally or unconditionally.

This is a useful exercise for you to undertake, so that you can see what, how, and why you feel the way you do about the word 'love' and how it manifests itself in your relationships with your partner, children, family, and friends.

The interpretation of love can be different for us all. Love doesn't necessarily have the same interpretation for each of us. There is no right and wrong just a different view on the word Love. Be clear in what you believe love is for you. You can, I am sure, recall the experience of the love you felt for your partner when you first met and leading up to the time that the betrayal took place. Ask yourself is your interpretation of love different now than from your original understanding of the word Love when you first became a couple?

Going forward after betrayal, what should you expect from each other in your future life together?

- You expect love and romance to last
- You expect to be understood
- You expect for both of you to compromise
- You expect to share your feelings with your partner
- You expect for you both to be respectful of each other's feelings
- You expect to have your sexual needs met
- You expect to have a comfortable life (financially)

Again, you can add to this list. How much of the above is realistic? In this 'going forward' stage your future relationship will be as you both want it to be as long as you both keep your needs, wants and desires in the forefront of your mind and remain committed.

Love comes in three stages:

1. Lust Stage:

This is the 'shopping' stage. This is the stage when you looked around trying to find 'the one'. This stage can start from 12 years of age and upwards.

2. Romantic stage:

This is when you 'bagged' your partner. This is when you believed you had found 'the one' and were enjoying the feelings in this early stage. You might have given each other gifts, you will probably have received loads of text messages, emails, or phone calls from your new partner and you both bathed in a cloud of loving during that time.

3. Attachment stage:

This is the 'routine' stage. It's when the two of you made the decision to marry or live together, had your children and worked to look after your family. (This is the stage when divorce rates are highest, and when 'betrayal' is most likely to occur). Other significant issues are brought into the equation during this time, i.e., bills to pay, deadlines to meet, parents/in-laws to take into consideration, children, work commitments, etc. It is at this point that disappointments occur and diversions take the focus away from your original plan.

In starting over and 'moving on' after betrayal you will need to discuss and address the following issues:

- You should discuss your expectations of each other
- You should discuss and decide your joint goals
- You should discuss how to cope with the inevitable difficulties and hurdles that will arise

- You should discuss that there will be changes in your relationship and both agree with the changes
- You should discuss and accept that life is no 'picnic'
- You should be fair and just with each other
- You should always practice putting your partner's needs first
- You should not blame your partner if you feel worthless
- You should accept that you are responsible for your own well-being
- You should expect to sacrifice some of your pleasures for the good of the relationship
- You should learn and accept each other's shortfalls.
- You should discuss and accept compromise
- You should both think before you react
- You should both risk letting your partner see who you really are
- You should structure your life together to include joint ventures or hobbies.

A good relationship takes a great deal of effort and energy to keep it burning at the right temperature. *'The path of true love does not run smooth.'* When you are 'moving on' after a betrayal, you will both need to stay focused on your path, always ensuring both your needs are met, by doing this you will have a better opportunity of securing a future for you both.

Your new relationship (after betrayal) should be based on the following suggestions:

- Respect for each other
- Appreciation of each other
- Acceptance of each other
- Understanding each other

The most satisfying intimate relationships are those that have open communication between each other and are mutually supportive, honest and realistic.

Step 4 Examining Partnership and Marriage

Marriage

A general definition of marriage is that it is a social contract between two individuals that unites their lives legally, economically and emotionally. Being married also gives legitimacy to sexual relations within the marriage. When a betrayal of trust is broken between two people, and both have decided to give the relationship a second chance, it is important to understand and see clearly the process of the marriage framework.

The most common stages of the marriage process are:

- Just married
- Parenting
- Empty nest
- Midlife
- Grandparenting
- Retirement
- Widow/Widower
- Life alone

If you understand the process a marriage goes through, then you will be better equipped to address the necessary changes that you will both need to make in 'moving on' together after a betrayal has occurred.

So, what should this strategy contain?

- Your hopes and dreams (however large or small) for your new future life together
- Your new expectations of each other

- Whether you intend moving house or staying put (some people prefer to move house after a betrayal in order to have a completely fresh start)
- Mutual finances (how should they be proportioned?)
- Mutual families (do you tell them of the betrayal — do they already know? Your strategy should say how you intend to deal with this issue).
- Hobbies and interests (both mutual and individual hobbies and interests)
- Career and educational opportunities (for both of you)
- Health Insurance (for the family)

Successful Marriages and Partnerships

Marriage has traditionally been understood as a social contract between a man (husband) and a woman (wife).

Successful marriages and partnerships are based on a solid emotional foundation. The range of emotional and physical states that a long-term marriage/partnership experiences will be exactly the same when you are 'moving on' from a betrayal. They are as follows:

- You make a decision to love one another
- You identify and arrange suitable financial arrangements
- You decide how frequently you visit your respective families
- You decide how to address family planning
- You decide how you will raise your children
- You decide who will do what in respect of domestic chores
- You discuss your sexual preferences

- You devise a strategy on how to address stress and pressure when it is present
- You discuss career decisions
- You will discuss and decide how to respect each others friends and hobbies

Types of Marriage

In today's modern world there exist different styles of marriage:

- Love matches
- Arranged marriages
- Remarriages
- Second, third, or later marriages
- Cousin marriage
- Same sex marriages
- Prison marriages (death row marriages)

In the 'moving on' stage of your relationship when you both decide that you want to try again you are essentially, re-forming a partnership. This new partnership should be equal, loving, and have healthy boundaries to allow for growth. To form a healthy partnership, you both need to share your innermost thoughts and feelings so that you can put together a mutually satisfying strategy that is based on the truth as both of you see it. It is essential that you both communicate to each other what exactly it is you want from your relationship after a betrayal has occurred.

Partnership

It is difficult to give a clear definition of a partnership, but the essential ingredients are:

- To achieve something you could not do alone
- To pool skills and other resources
- To have a shared vision of your goals

- To work together to reach your goals
- To devise a long-term formal structure
- To devise a short-term agreement

The benefits of a business partnership are as follows:

- To share ideas
- To share joint finances
- To be aware of joint ambitions
- To bring two sets of skills into the partnership
- To be supportive, loyal and committed
- To learn to see things through someone else's eyes

When both partners work toward the same objective, it can be achieved faster than doing it alone. The joining of the marriage criteria and the business partnership criteria make for a substantial foundation for your new future together. If it is possible to stick to the agreed points on both fronts, then you will both have planned for a future to look forward to.

On your journey through your life, you can, and probably already have, encountered major problems.

Here are some negative examples:

- The possibility of bankruptcy
- The possibility of infidelity/Betrayal
- The possibility of illness (parents or children)
- The possibility of losing your job
- The possibility of financial difficulties
- The possibility of sexual problems
- The possibility of irreconcilable opinions
- The possibility of extended family disputes
- The possibility of early death

I am sure you can think of many more. Why don't you both use this opportunity to go back in your memory and talk over some of the difficult experiences you have already survived together? See this step as an opportunity to reevaluate the decisions you both arrived at during those stressful times. Ask each other, 'if the same experience recurred now, would your answer be different?' Remember we are all wise in hindsight.

Step 5   Understanding Disappointments

Disappointment in marriage/partnership

When you first got together, you were probably full of hopes and expectations for your future life together. As your relationship developed, you should have gained trust in one another. You should have become friends, companions as well as lovers. During this early part of your marriage/partnership you probably would have planned how and what you both wanted for your life together. Dreams and aspirations are hatched during this time. As you now know, it was important then to make your aspirations, hopes and dreams realistic and attainable and any good plan would have identified and set targets along the way to achieving your aim. Look back, was your plan realistic? Did you have a plan? Whatever the answer, the same rule applies now when you are 'moving on after betrayal'. It is important to understand that if this new plan is far fetched and unrealistic, this will have a detrimental effect on each of you as the pressure increases while you try to reach unattainable targets.

Each and every one of us enters into a relationship with a set of skills (practical and emotional).

Practical skills

- Do-it-yourself skills
- Cooking
- Household Management
- Home Decorating/Maintenance
- Gardening
- Driving

- Career
- Nurturing

I am sure you can add to this list of examples. The above is a small selection.

Emotional Skills

- Listening
- Talking
- Problem Solving
- Loving
- Communication skills
- Forgiving

- Understanding
- Leadership skills
- Truth/Honesty
- Able to say sorry
- Passionate

I am sure that you can think of more. For many of you, looking at this list of emotional skills, it might identify that you entered into your earlier relationship completely ignorant of the most basic requirements needed to fulfill any objectives and expectations you both might have aspired to. Don't worry if this is the case, most of us enter relationships completely ignorant of these most basic facts. Here is an example:

A woman who was referred to me with relationship problems told me that if only she had known that her partner's verbal and practical skills were so limited, she would have walked away from the relationship before it started. She said that, "For the first two years of the marriage her husband had lived up to her expectations of what he could do", then, she says, "He ran out of steam and became apathetic and verbally redundant." When she confronted him regarding this issue, he told her that he hated fixing things around the house and also that he felt that because of his job, he was a salesman, that he didn't want to talk when he arrived home as he had been talking all day and that she should understand that he was fed up having to talk to her in the evenings.

Why are we so blinded by love?

In order for you to avoid disappointment in your 'going forward' relationship, it is vital that you both understand and accept your strengths and weaknesses. By understanding each other's **strengths** and **weaknesses** you will be able to forgive and 'move on' more easily. Good communication between couples is an essential element to a good relationship. If one partner feels unable to confide in the other, or discuss important issues with their partner, then, eventually, the relationship will start to crumble. Keep your expectations of your partner realistic. Remember, no-one is super-human.

Let's take a look at some common situations between people that highlight poor communication skills:

- When your significant other does all the talking and doesn't give you an opportunity to give your point of view

- When you first got together you were talking all the time but now you don't have anything to say to one another

- When your partner says that you are not hearing what s/he is saying and calls you stupid

- When you are afraid to tell your partner how you feel because you are afraid of the angry retort

- When you reach a certain point in the argument your partner always threatens to walk out and leave you

- When you are afraid to talk too much in case you come to the conclusion that there is nothing left in your relationship.

Achieving a successful relationship and safeguarding against disappointment requires some skill and a lot of tenacity. It is challenging. Most people don't understand that skills are required to promote a successful relationship. Often, one partner identifies this fact and the other partner is in blissful ignorance.

You should really begin learning about your future partner from your first meeting. However, after living through the bitter experience of betrayal, you have the opportunity to update your knowledge about your partner.

Remember, when you chose your partner, you chose a way of life. What do you now need to find out?

- How your partner thinks?
- How your partner communicates?
- What hurts your partner?
- What type of humor does your partner appreciate?
- What is your partner's taste in food, etc?
- What are your partner's dislikes?
- Is your partner responsible for their actions and speech?
- Is your partner passionate?
- Has your partner got common interests and goals?
- Do you like your partner?
- Has your partner got any hidden agendas?
- Is your partner good with money issues?

All these questions will help you both to see if you are still compatible. You don't want a carbon copy of yourself, I know. You are, however, deciding to 'move forward' and have decided to share the rest of your lives together. It is important, therefore, to take everything (the exchanges, disagreements, etc) that you have identified very seriously. These exchanges and responses will be the blueprint your new relationship will be based on. A common fault in relationships is make excuses for your partner. You still probably don't want to believe that your partner is difficult/not responding/always wants their own way etc. You want to believe that the last remark/issue was an oversight on their part and not the way they would respond normally.

Excuses! You need to 'get real' and see exactly how your partner interacts with you, and others you both come in contact with. Listen to yourself and take note of your 'gut' reaction (intuition) to what is happening. Your perceptions are seldom wrong. Know it, and make it work for you. In the past, you might have convinced yourself that you could change your partner. Now you understand and accept that you can only change you. The big question is, 'are you prepared to change and compromise, and is your partner prepared to change and compromise?' Some people don't believe they need to change, they think they are perfect. No-one is perfect. No-one wants to unearth faults in themselves or in their chosen partner. But you both have to be realistic and learn from the mistakes you have made. We all have the capacity to re-learn skills and to establish positive patterns of behavior instead of the negative patterns we have always used.

Suggestions to take on how to 'move forward' to a mutually satisfying relationship:

- The relationship should be your safe haven from the world
- Positive behavior should be identified by both of you and encouraged
- Negative behavior should be identified by both of you and discouraged.

- Make sure that you replace the negative behavior with a positive behavior

- Learn how to disagree without falling out with each other

- Learn how to behave appropriately rather than instinctually

- Be ready to talk and listen to your partner.

The adult skills you now have come from your childhood relationships formed with your parents, aunts, uncles, grandparents. These people were your early role-models. You may not have learned communication skills, honesty and acceptance. Don't forget we all come from dysfunctional families. You are no different than the next person.

Decide to change your thought processes and install positive thinking and new behavior patterns in your mind.

You can do this by:

- Being optimistic and positive about your relationship

- Creating a safety net for you both, and support each other through a process of change

- Being tolerant and understanding and not expecting too much too soon

- Knowing that there will be disagreements. Make a decision to change the way you both behave when this happens. Form an agreement with your partner that if one of you fails to adhere to the agreement you have drawn up, then the one who cannot connect walks away from the argument for the time being

- Preventing an argument from spiraling out of control and causing serious long-term damage. Go for damage limitation and stop the argument before it gets a life of its own. Walk away, calm down, think things through and decide on a more appropriate, reasonable response

- Remembering you can disagree without throwing insults at one another

- Remembering silence can be worse than anger

- Avoid apportioning 'blame'

- Understanding that no one is asking that you change your characteristics and personality. The issue is to learn or re-learn communication and problem solving skills

- Reminding yourselves every morning that you are both committed to changing your patterns

- Congratulating yourselves each evening when you have fulfilled your agreement

This list can act as a new strategy, or blueprint, for 'moving on after betrayal' in order to remind you of your commitment to love one another through good and bad times in the future.

Step 6   Creating Expectations and Boundaries

Your future depends on what you **expect** from life. **When you choose a partner you are not just choosing a person you are choosing 'a way of life.'** How many of you think of that fact when you begin a relationship?

It's important that you both have the same expectations when you begin this new phase of your life together. It's important to share your innermost thoughts and feelings with your partner. Expectations come from your own previous experiences (both as a child and as an adult), and the experiences that your childhood friends have shared with you regarding their expectations, i.e. "What do you want to be when you grow up?" Your expectations will also stem from observing the inter-actions of your parents, grandparents, uncles, aunts, teachers and older children you admire. These non-verbal messages are stored in your unconscious mind to use when an appropriate time arises, i.e., dating/ marriage/ living together/daily interactions.

Your choice of partner reflects who you are. If you choose a partner when you are feeling low/ depressed / unhappy/ disillusioned, then it is possible that your partner will reflect some of those emotions. It's the synchronicity that draws people to each other. I am sure that you have heard the expression, 'like attracts like'. The patterns of thoughts and behavior that have been imprinted in your memory box, from your childhood, will attract those people to you that will enable these established patterns of behavior to regurgitate so that you can 'dance to the old familiar tune' of responses that you know so well. This is an automatic response that unconsciously links you to people who can trigger off these firmly placed patterns. If your established patterns of behavior are based on negative experiences, then you will attract people to you that will compound your early negative belief system.

You have to fully understand and accept the circumstances and concept of loving someone you have decided to 'move on' with.

Previous relationships that failed

- Were you in the right frame of mind when making the decision to commit to your ex-partner?
- Did any of your previous partners reflect your early negative emotional belief system?
- Can you identify that your circumstances and responses mirrored past experiences?

All your emotional experiences are lessons to be learned. The best lessons are the ones that have hurt you at the time, but have now recovered from.

Are there boundaries in your relationship?

I think of boundaries as invisible lines I cannot cross. What are the limits you are prepared to go to in getting what you want?

Here are several ways in which your boundaries, or lack of them, can cause problems. I will explain each of them:

- Strong desire to be needed
- A lack of identity
- Believing that everything is my fault
- Believing that everything is your fault

- Believing that everything will be alright in the end
- Being helpless, a poor me, a victim
- Being frivolous in spending money
- Living your life through your partner
- A fear of outcomes that your partner will not like
- Engaging in misplaced guilt
- A belief of never feeling good enough

Strong desire to be needed (Negative)

Some people feel that they are nothing without a significant other. You could change every aspect of yourself in order to accommodate your partner—I know many people who have done this including me—but unfortunately to no avail. All personal development change in thought, speech and behavior must be done by you. If you change to accommodate your partner, then you are denying your own strengths, character and personality to develop and mature. Women are masters at changing themselves to accommodate a partner. Many women are chameleons, who can change their behavior in order to get someone to like them. You can become too flexible and adaptable to please your partner. This can cause you to suffer anxiety and depression at a later date, when you become totally encapsulated and imprisoned in the persona you have created for yourself. Ask yourself, 'am I being used as scaffolding to keep my partner upright?' 'Is my partner a parasite?' In other words, is s/he sucking the very substance of life out of you in order to reign supreme? If this is the case then this relationship is unhealthy and stunting for the dependent partner and a great load to place on the dominant partner.

Strong desire to be needed (Positive)

You do not need anyone to validate you. You are whole as you are. Remember, you managed you life prior to meeting your present partner. Start building your self-confidence by joining a group, developing a hobby, meeting with positive friends, become employed (full or part-time), re-train, etc. A healthy relationship shares some interests and hobbies with their partner whilst being able to develop independently also.

Lack of identity

- Is your identity linked to your partner's identity?
- Do you feel you are nothing without your partner?
- Are you willing to do anything to make the relationship work?
- Are you prepared to give everything up for your partner?
- Do you think it is better to stay in your relationship and feel lost and scared, rather than be on your own?
- Have you become too dependent on your partner?
- Do you believe this relationship is right for you?

These are the questions you should ask yourself. Any change you have made in your behavior in order to accommodate your partner is the act of denying who you are, and accepting that the 'real' you is of no value. When this happens you unconsciously put yourself and your feelings down. You are ignoring your basic needs. In order to survive and strive for a healthy future relationship, you need to have good self-esteem, and value yourself, before you value anyone else.

> "Everything you need you already have. You are complete right now; you are a whole, total person, not an apprentice person on the way to someplace else."   —Wayne Dyer

Being an independent person in your relationship can have mutual benefits. Both of you are able to understand and identify the differences between you and celebrate them. A loving couple should bring different positive attributes into a relationship.

You are adults and should know when you are crossing an agreed upon boundary. If this happens, then own it, and change your pattern. It is immature to have an agreed boundary and forget it, if and when you want to, in order to prove a point or get your own way. It is important that you both recognize when you fall into bad patterns/habits and are able to change your ways to accommodate each other. This is an essential element in 'moving on'.

Everything is my fault

If you have changed and become the image your partner has projected on to you in order to cope and survive within your relationship, then you have done the following:

- Said "Sorry" when you were not to blame
- Assumed responsibility, so as not to put your partner under extra pressure
- Catered to your partner's every whim
- Put yourself down so that the other person can 'lord it over you'
- Changed so much of yourself that you don't recognize yourself anymore

- Acted as moderator between your partner and your children
- Put up with your partner's tantrums
- Made excuses for your partner's behavior to others
- Engineered every conversation so that your partner could look good
- Made your close family and close friends aware of how difficult your partner has been, and counted on their loyalty to you to put up with your partner
- Distanced yourself from the opinion of others

The list, once again, is endless and unique to each of us. These scenarios are acted out by someone desperate to have their partner stay in the relationship at any cost. Please remember that however much you change yourself, it will never be enough. You will continually be trying to keep up with how the other person wants you to be.

Everything will be alright in the end

Does everything turn out alright in the end? Think about it. Go back in your memory and discover if all the things you have changed about you have made any difference to the way your partner has behaved toward you and others. The answer is NO. You or your partner's behavior might have modified for some of the time, but only for short periods until the wave of hysteria, anger, manipulation and control has returned to imprison you or your partner even further.

The only way to make everything alright in the end is to set about making slow, positive, subtle changes to the way you interact with each other. This should be done carefully, over a long period of time. This exercise is hard to do initially, but the results at the end can be tremendous.

Knowing the difference between love and pity

Do you look at your partner, sometimes, and feel a surge of pity? I am sure the answer to this question is YES. You have a desire to help this person to see things differently and more logically. The warm feeling that this pity generates might make you think that you are still in love with your partner. You try to understand what motivates your partner's behavior. Here are some of the excuses you will discover:

- A bad experience with a previous partner
- A bad relationship with parents
- The fear of losing control over you, resulting in you leaving
- The fear of losing self-control
- The fear of your partner finding out that you are cleverer that h/she is (women, particularly, do this when they feel they need to boost the ego of their partner)

Healthy boundaries in healthy relationships

- To celebrate yourself as an independent person
- To know, understand and talk together when either of you is 'crossing the line' (boundary)
- To be able to share financial commitments
- To accept you are in the wrong when you are
- To be ready, willing, and able to say you are sorry
- To be able to agree on time limits regarding outside activities (visits to in-laws, friends, etc.)
- To be able to agree on boundaries that enable further education. This allows you to develop a career and helps you to focus on yourself
- To ensure you set aside time to be with each other

Make your own list of what healthy boundaries you both want in your relationship.

Helplessness

The 'helpless' person is the 'victim' or the 'poor me'. If you are this person, you feel weak and vulnerable due to the pressures placed on you by your partner. Their expectations of you are too demanding and are depleting your inner resources. Some partners are good at presenting to you their inability to deal with any type of issue that arises. This requires you to step in and rescue your partner, and deal with all and sundry. This might temporarily make you feel good. You will spend a considerable amount of time teaching and helping your partner to deal with life. If they know how and what to do and choose not to do it because they know you will do it for them, then this is a conscious deception on their part. This might occur, of course, but an unconscious, gradual shifting of the load is more likely.

The 'poor me' person is not deceiving the other partner any more than they are deceiving themselves. They opt out. They are just being lazy. You are the proverbial 'fish on the hook'. Once again, you have succumbed to manipulation. You are, or have been, controlled all of the time. Helplessness is a learned behavior. Remember there are advantages to being helpless and one of them is that the helpless person does much less than a self-reliant one does. One of the reasons someone is helpless is because they are afraid of an outcome that will put their partner in a bad mood and the situation will end up with the breakup of the relationship. It is like the 'Sword of Damocles' constantly hovering above your head. Some people live in this way for years. It is awful. It causes problems. You feel there is no escape. You feel trapped in your love for your partner. Ask yourself, 'is this love?'

Frivolous spending

What is frivolous spending?

- Purchasing unnecessary items to make you feel good about yourself

- Purchasing an item in order to 'make things better'

- Buying 'special food' to show how much you care

- Going into debt to ensure your partner gets is always satisfied

- Spending money behind your partner's back

All the above, and more, is frivolous spending. It is important for both of you to budget your finances for your new future together. The first step in achieving this is to decide to arrange Direct Debits from your bank to pay for regular services that are in your home, i.e., gas, electricity, mortgage, telephone bills, insurance policies, council taxes, etc. If you haven't already put this in place, do it now. In doing this you will know exactly how much money you both have left in the bank each month. Any purchases made after this should be mutually agreed upon. If you are living with a 'control freak,' this person will want total control of the finances. Having total control of the finances makes your partner feel safe and secure. It leaves you, however, having to ask or beg for every cent you need to purchase any personal items, e.g. gifts and even toiletries.

Financial affairs

Financial affairs should be mutually accepted between you. Design a jointly suitable financial budget. Anything over and above that should be agreed on by both. Consider whether you have a dependency on your partner to live your life:

- Have you done this?

- Why do you do this?

- Didn't you manage your life well prior to meeting your partner?

- Are you seriously thinking that you cannot manage to live your life alone?

- Ask yourself what function does this person have in your life that you believe enables you?

This person has destroyed your confidence and has, therefore, made you emotionally redundant. Do you need or want that to happen to you or to continue happening to you? Let's look at these things that bind you to your partner:

- You cannot pay the bills alone

- You cannot raise the children alone

- You are afraid of being on your own

- You don't know enough about insurances, taxes, cars, etc.

- You need emotional support

- You need to be loved

- You need to share your life with someone or, dare I say, anyone

- You have outstanding debts that you cannot pay alone

- You cannot do the DIY jobs that are necessary to keep your home running smoothly

- You don't want to rely on family to help you

- You are scared of what people (generally) might say.

This is another exhaustive list that is unique to each of us. You are imprisoning yourself. Be realistic about the things that you feel have bound you to your partner. Decide to learn how to tackle one of the above examples. This will help you realize that, in fact, you can do stuff you thought you were unable to achieve alone. This exercise will boost the morale and confidence of the 'helpless' partner.

It is necessary to go through this process of looking at what has bound you to your partner so that you will not make the mistake of 'moving on' together because you are afraid to go it alone! The more able partner will see the benefit of your efforts to learn new things and should encourage your efforts.

Know your limitations in how much you can take on.

Learn to say 'no' when appropriate. If something isn't appropriate, it is inappropriate. Use this sentence as a yardstick in order to identify how much energy you can give to outside interests. The first thing on your agenda should be to make time to be with each other. However, we all need to recharge our batteries and re-energize in order to continue communicating at a healthy, acceptable, normal level. Be focused and re-invest in your relationship at every opportunity.

Fear of an outcome that your partner would not like

In the past in order to assuage your partner, you will have made sure that the outcome of any situation would suit that person. You might have, or had, 'some' control over domestic issues, but have, or had, no control over your partner's professional life. You will, or are already finding, that one spills over to the other. This means that, however well you manage your domestic problems and outcomes, you cannot manage or control the outcome or issue that arises in your partner's workplace. You are, therefore, in a no win situation. If your partner reacts to problems either at home or work by attacking you (using you as a whipping boy), then you are dealing with someone who is emotionally immature. (I am sure that you know that already). There is no easy way out of this situation.

The fear of a negative outcome is so frightening that you might have allowed yourself to be sucked dry by your partner in the hope that this will make that person feel better." The only way forward is to let go of trying to save your significant other and start looking after you by re-acting in a different, more subtle manner (as outlined in my book *'MY WAY' to help you live in a difficult relationship*). Unfortunately, if you are the dominant partner you will have to watch your partner struggle with problems in order to give them space for their own personal growth. Don't be hoodwinked and held to ransom. Understand the 'emotional blackmail' that could be taking place so that you will take over. 'Tough love' is to allow a person to grow and heal through becoming self-reliant. It is the opposite of 'carrying that person'.

Misplaced guilt

Here are some examples of the guilt you might feel:

- When you believe you owe your partner a place to live
- When you believe you owe your partner for paying bills
- When you believe you owe your partner for helping out with children of the partnership
- When you believe you should allow your partner to use your home as a venue when s/he has access to your children

This is baloney. You could, I am sure, manage on your own if necessary. Decide to choose to stay in the relationship because you want to and not because you believe you think you need to. Some partners are very good at playing mind games. Mind games are unconscious games people play in order to gain control over another person. Another word to use, which means the same, is 'hidden agendas'. It is 'mind games' and 'hidden agendas' that form part of the core of 'betrayal'

Step 7   Learning Responsibility

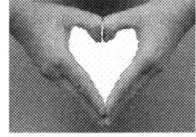

As stated in previous Steps, in order to 'move on' after a betrayal has taken place you will both need to reassess and re-establish the foundation of your relationship. You can do this by following the process.

The first task is to understand and accept 'responsibility'. I intend to explain 'personal responsibility' in more detail later on as this type of responsibility needs to be affirmed for a couple' moving on' after a betrayal has taken place.

How many types of responsibility are there?

- Personal responsibility
- Relationship Responsibility (accepting your individual roles and the responsibility that accompanies your role)
- Financial Responsibility (to be careful and budget wisely)
- Social/Community responsibility (to ensure you behave appropriately at all times)
- Professional Responsibility (to say what you do and do what you say)
- Family Responsibility (watching out for children and aged parents or relatives)
- Responsibility for your speech and actions (if something said or done isn't pertinent it's impertinent)
- Educational Responsibility (ensuring satisfactory education for your children, or indeed, of either partner)

- Responsibility for your health (regular health screening, etc)
- Moral Responsibility (you are the role models for your children-they will copy your behavior—remember it!)

Well-balanced Relationship Responsibility:

All adults are 100% responsible for who they are and what they do. Each adult is 50% responsible in a relationship. Each adult is 0% responsible for any other person (adult)

- To be reliable, loyal and dependable, whatever it is you have agreed to accomplish do it and don't shirk this responsibility and expect others to do your allotted tasks
- To take full responsibility for your speech and actions
- To think before you speak. (Consider the reactions of others to what you say and do).

Unbalanced Relationship Responsibility Indications:

- When you are unable to say 'no' to anyone
- When you are emotionally 'cut off' from your relationship with your partner
- When you are unable to take criticism
- When you are violent, intimidating and threatening behavior (physical or emotional)
- When you are making sure someone else is happy— neglecting yourself in the process
- When you have no power/control in a relationship
- When you are being a 'victim'
- When you are unable to be clear about what you are saying when in discussion with your partner (emotionally disabled)

What is Personal Responsibility?

- You are accountable for your actions

- You are accountable for your thoughts (negative or positive)

- You are accountable for your choices

- You are accountable for your career

- You are accountable for your mistakes

- No one is to blame for who or what you have become—just you

- You are only responsible for yourself and the adult you have become

- You are accountable for you emotions, health and general well-being

- You are accountable for whatever life has thrown at you and it is your responsibility to accept and own that fact.

> "My philosophy is that not only are you responsible for your life, but doing the best at this moment puts you in the best place for the next moment."
> —Oprah Winfrey

These are some of the sayings that you hear from people who have opted out of accepting responsibility:

- There's a black cloud hanging over my head
- Nothing good ever happens to me
- It's not my luck
- It isn't my fault I am like this
- I didn't ask to be born
- Why doesn't anything good ever happen to me?
- I'm too old to change
- It's the way I was brought up

- Stop the world, I want to get off.

What do you call people who 'opt out' of taking personal responsibility?

- Victims
- Martyrs
- Lazy
- Depressed
- Moaners

- Hostile
- Neurotic
- Inferiority Complex
- Pessimists

How can you change and start taking responsibility?

- **Listen to your inner dialogue** and change the pattern of thought from negative to positive. Write your negative thoughts down and change them to the opposite positive thought. Be determined to change all negative actions and reactions

- **Stop all spontaneous reactions**. By doing this you will stop yourself repeating the old bad patterns that slip off your tongue. Don't react. Stop and think before you speak. This will be difficult to achieve at first but with practice it will become second nature to you

- **Let go of past emotions:** hurt, anger, guilt, insecurity, mistrust, fears, and blame. Tell yourself you are fed up with regurgitating the same old stuff. In doing this simple exercise you will be consciously and unconsciously re-programming your negative mind chatter to positive mind chatter

- **Overcome your fears** by facing them and working through them. Nothing is as bad as you imagine it to be. Remember the slogan, 'face the fear and the fear will disappear'.

- **Start believing in yourself:** You can be and do anything you put your mind to

- **Focus on your strengths:** build upon them to raise your self-esteem

- **Start believing in your dreams:** set about making them happen

- **Start taking risks:** you won't get anywhere standing still. Life is about taking risks!

- **Share your problems** with a trusted friend/counselor. These people will be objective to your situation which will help you to clear your mind of unnecessary dross

- **Be open-minded** and engage in honest communication

- Believe in, and live the slogan, **'If it's meant to be, it's up to me'**

- **Widen your vision**: start seeing the opportunities that are there for you

- **Remember you are in charge** of your life and direction it takes.

All the above suggestions and exercises are necessary to complete, in order for you both to understand each other and communicate with honesty. The person who has been betrayed will have experienced the devastating effect of the crumbling foundations of their relationship and the personal humiliation and shame that a betrayal brings. The betrayer should be repentant and eager to establish honest communication. The foundation of your relationship is a pivotal part in starting over.

> "We are made wise not by the recollection of our past, but by the responsibility for our future."
> —George Bernard Shaw

Step 8 Managing Jealousy and Control

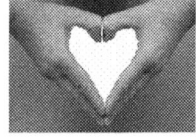

First of all let's take a look at jealousy. Jealousy displays itself through unhappiness and anger because someone has something you want, or because you think that someone might take something or someone that you love away from you. Jealousy in an intimate relationship can cause a major rift. Sometimes betrayal occurs when one partner is over-possessive of the other partner.

What Jealous People Say:

- "My mother was always jealous of my father"
- "I don't trust anyone"
- "My parents let me down"
- "I am jealous of my partner's ex's"
- "My partner lied to me about an ex"
- "My partner looks at 'porn'"
- "I catch my partner looking at other women/men"
- "I am jealous of the people my partner works with"
- "He/she keeps photographs of his ex's"
- "I have seen him/her flirt"

How is jealousy portrayed?

- Complete indifference
- Inability to control thoughts, words, deeds
- Destructive behavior
- Displays of unreasonableness
- Being suspicious
- Continual questioning
- Self indulgence
- Being helpless

- Being a victim/poor me
- Anger/frustration
- Being vulnerable
- Feeling rejected
- Feeling insecure

What can be done to overcome jealousy?

The simple answer to this question is, by **TRUSTING.** If you believe that you cannot trust your partner. Perhaps you need to gather evidence to substantiate your belief before confronting your partner.

In order to move on after a betrayal, trust is an essential element in re-building your personal relationship. The betrayal occurred because one partner took advantage of the other partner's belief that they could be trusted. In 'moving on' trust is the part of the relationship that must come before anything else. If you cannot trust your partner then you have to face the possibility that the relationship will end.

What is Trust?

'To have **belief** or **confidence** in the honesty, goodness, skill, or safety of a person.'

In order to overcome jealousy, you must trust yourself before you trust others. Trusting yourself means valuing yourself and your abilities. If you have a low self-esteem/self-worth, this feeling can lead to being jealous of your partner as you don't believe you are worthy of love or faithfulness from anyone. Your past experiences in relationships also are the cause for jealousy in your present relationship. If your parents abandoned you, either physically or emotionally, you will expect nothing better from anyone else. If your ex broke your trust by being unfaithful to you, then you will feel frightened to trust someone else in case they do the same.

Also, you will attract people to you that will enable you to replay your old negative script. You will feel temporarily safe when this happens because you will know what to say and how to behave when you meet someone that links you into your old bad script habit. Recognize the signs, if this occurs. You will be able to identify them because you will know that you have said the same statements to other people all of your life.

Be alert to the things you say, and if you are repeating thought and speech patterns, then you should stop and change your thinking, speech and behavior as I have shown you in Step 7. Don't bring your old routine and baggage into a new relationship. You should not ruin your present relationship, and judge your present partner, on any past relationship you have experienced. Individuals who are jealous are usually aware of this problem, but can't help themselves. The facts are that you don't know anything with a 100% guarantee. Without a guarantee you are unable to trust. It's a vicious circle of unhappiness and discontent.

Jealous people protect themselves from possible hurt, disappointment, rejection and pain by guarding themselves and withdrawing into their own cocoon of safety. Unfortunately, when this happens, they are pushing their partners away from them. **You must choose to love, believe, accept and trust someone.** I have seen many marriages/partnerships crumble because one of the partners is unable to take the leap from distrust to trust. You can bring about your worst fears by projecting your fears on to your partner. Stop this behavior before it is too late.

Jealousy is based in insecurity and fear. You are frightened to let your partner come too close to you in fear of you becoming too vulnerable. You believe that 'as you are' will not be enough to keep your partner interested in you. You believe this because of your past experiences in relationships. This results in you trying to become the person you think your partner wants to be with. You are afraid of showing the 'real you' in case you are not what your partner wants. Partnership/Marriage is based on emotional intimacy. This is an essential ingredient required for the relationship to grow and mature. Without emotional intimacy you will have a superficial relationship that cannot be maintained. Emotional intimacy between two people who love each other is a fulfilling loving experience. By continuing to be as you are (jealous) you are denying yourself the feeling of this over-powering, satisfying emotion. Emotional intimacy will only grow by knowing you are totally acceptable to your partner the way you are.

Steps to Stop Being Jealous

- Stop questioning your partner: walk away if you feel you are about to do this. Go to another room and think carefully about what would happen if you did question your partner. Remember that their reply will only give you temporary relief. You have done it before, and you know it will not last. So don't do it.

- Remind yourself of how loving your partner is. Recognize how much this person does for you. Be realistic and ask yourself what evidence you have to reach the conclusion that your partner cannot be trusted

- When you hear yourself (inner dialogue) thinking your old worn-out thought patterns, tell yourself 'not to go there.' Do not listen to this old record in your memory. Stay in the here and now and focus on what is real. (Go back to Step 7 and re-read 'changing your patterns of behavior). You are in a loving relationship

- Jealousy says more about you than your partner. Improve your self-esteem (as shown in Step 2). Distract yourself from these damaging thoughts by engaging in something positive for you

- 'Life is about taking risks.' You have to step 'out of the field of poppies' and take a risk in life. Share your thoughts and feelings about yourself with your partner. Don't be afraid to show your vulnerability. Together you may be able to find a way to erase these irrational feelings

- If you find all these things too difficult to handle alone, go to your General Practitioner and ask to be referred to a Counselor/Therapist who will help you with these issues.

Jealousy and Control

To live your life under someone else's control is mind-numbing. It not only destroys you, it destroys your relationship. Destructive behavior such as jealousy, deception and betrayal can occur if one partner controls the other. The stifling feeling of being controlled sometimes pushes the victim to seek emotional support elsewhere.

If you have been or, are being, controlled by your partner, you are feeling:

- Powerless
- Lethargic
- Undermined
- Intimidated
- Angry
- Hostile
- Resentful
- Unworthy

- Lacking in self-esteem
- Ugly
- Useless
- As if you couldn't do anything right
- Bullied
- Destroyed
- Over-whelmed by negativity
- Drained of energy.

And many more feelings that are unique to each of us.

Following on from jealousy is **Control** which is common in relationships and usually happens when jealousy is present. If you are jealous of your partner and feel compelled to control this person, then this would highlight your own lack of security, identity and self-worth. You are controlling someone because you are jealous of your partner and insecure in the relationship. This insecurity might have started during your childhood. Perhaps you were neglected/ignored/abused/or even over-indulged. Controllers take charge quickly, choosing to rise above their emotional pain, instead of feeling the pain themselves and working through the emotion.

Controllers are arrogant and justify their behavior by convincing their victim that they are always right, and by projecting threatening behavior.

Here are some examples of what a controller might say:

- You are nothing without me
- You are weak
- You could never manage living alone
- "I've made you what you are"
- "If it wasn't for me, I don't know what would happen to you" (implying something lowly and negative)

- "I put up with you"
- "I feel sorry for you"
- "I love you dearly, but I do not fancy you" (patronizing)
- You've done it now. I didn't want to tell you the truth not to hurt you (Yeah, right)! but now you have forced my hand
- "You push me to behave in this way"
- "It's your fault"
- "That's me, if you don't like it—leave"

And loads more.

How many ways you can control someone:

- Financially (you hold the purse strings)
- Sexually (withdrawing from your partner physically and emotionally)
- Temper tantrums
- Demanding behavior
- Moody and sulking
- Possessiveness
- Violence
- Jealousy
- Bouts of crying
- Being helpless
- Manipulation

Control's foundation is fear. You are afraid that your partner might:

- Meet someone else
- Find you out!
- Divorce you

- Get a better job than you
- Have more friends than you
- Be liked more than you are
- Earn more money than you
- Be better looking than you
- Age better than you

Again, the list is endless.

How can you change someone who controls you?

You can't! The only person you can change is you. You have no control over someone else's behavior. They have to take personal responsibility for themselves and admit they are a controller and try to identify the root of the behavior they are caught up in and are continually repeating.

However, it takes two people to continue the negative process of controlling. The one doing the controlling, and the **'VICTIM'**.

Here are more examples that you can try in order to change your controlling patterns:

- Identify the triggers that start the control cycle
- Talk with your partner and share your feelings. You might need your partner's help with identifying exactly what sets you off
- Once you have identified the triggers, you can set about changing your attitude towards them
- Be realistic
- Stay focused on understanding that your reactions to the triggers are harmful to both of you
- Trust your partner
- Learn to have faith in each other
- Compromise when necessary

- Find alternative responses

- Put yourself to the test

- Be open with your partner and you will gain the support you need

In most relationships, one partner leads and the other follows. This is healthy leadership that has been agreed, either verbally or non-verbally, between you. In healthy relationships, either person can take control at any time without adverse reaction by the other partner. Both partners in the relationship feel equal whilst each partner retains the individual uniqueness that applies to each of us.

Control is 'learned behavior.' You were not born jealous. You were not born a controller. You have learned this behavior, so, therefore, you can unlearn it.

Step 9   Moving Forward From Betrayal

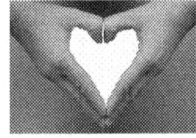

Now here comes the big question. Having read this book this far do you think that you 'can you move on after being betrayed?' The answer is yes. In order to do this, you have to accept the fact that you were partly responsible for the betrayal and engage in the difficult process of re-building your relationship as I have already outlines. Betrayal is a difficult thing to accept and overcome, and many can't and won't do it. You have to be fully aware of why the betrayal happened.

Here are some examples of why the betrayal happened:

- Your partner is a serial adulterer
- You both ignored the warning signs
- One or both of you became too embroiled in the children of the relationship
- One or both of you became too comfortable in your rut
- Neither of you fulfilled the criteria in the partnership/ marriage
- You didn't spend enough quality time with each other
- You didn't listen to each other
- One or both of you put too much emphasis on career
- Lack of communication
- Lack of intimacy.

When you have established why the betrayal took place, you are armed with essential information and can adopt strategies to ensure that this painful period won't be replicated.

Everyone at some time in their life has searched for the perfect relationship: the 'pot of gold at the end of the rainbow.' There isn't one. All relationships have their down side. We all have a set of problems (baggage) and a set of established skills, which we bring with us into our relationship. The trick is to find someone with a set of problems you can deal with, and a set of skills that are complementary to your own set of skills.

Relationships are not set in stone. Problems occur sometimes when one partner expects too much of the other one and becomes disappointed and frustrated when that person does not meet their expectations. All relationships are based on your belief in yourself. What, and who we are is brought into the loving relationship and if the relationship is rigid and taut, then there will be no flexibility and you will be unable to compromise. Remember you are a single, unique unit trying to live with another single, unique unit. By remembering this, you will understand the need to be open-minded, non-judgmental, and accepting of the huge differences between you. Once you understand that there is far more to you than you had thought, you will begin to understand why relationships are as they are–difficult. To be able to compromise is essential in a healthy relationship. You cannot agree all the time. When you don't agree, you should both be able to come to a compromise on how you should proceed.

We are what our internal dialogue says we are. We all talk to ourselves silently most of the time. Don't worry, this is normal. Our internal dialogue shows us how we view ourselves. If your 'mind chatter' has been negative this will affect your self confidence and self-esteem. If our internal dialogue is negative, and the pattern of our thinking says that we are unable to form relationships, then we won't form them. It's that simple! Your internal dialogue is an important aspect of who you are. If you feel that your internal dialogue is full of misgivings, begin the process of changing your thinking. Internal dialogue should be hopeful, clear, positive and realistic.

Do you feel responsible for someone else's emotions?

- Are you living in turmoil?
- Are you under pressure?
- Are you feeling drained?
- Are you lacking in energy?
- Are you undervalued?
- Are you being ignored?
- Are you lacking in interest?
- Are you comfort-eating?
- Are you suffering from disturbed sleep?
- Are you suffering from problems with concentration?
- Are you depressed?
- Are you anxious?

If you can identify with some the above, then it follows that you are feeling trapped with no visible escape.

When you decide to reconcile after a betrayal, it is the right time to examine all your disabling emotions. These emotions camouflage the real problem, which is 'lack of understanding and lack of **real** communication.'

Avoid responsibility for someone else's emotions

- Start keeping a diary and be meticulous, writing down how, why, and what you are feeling. Do this on a regular basis and, soon, a pattern will emerge that will identify the problematic areas that need changing

- Be brave and own your fears. Face them and they will go away

- Talk these problems over with your partner and, together, find solutions

- Acknowledge the triggers that set you both off down the path of despair and hopelessness

- Decide on how you are going to move forward with these problems

- Write down what you are responsible for. Encourage your partner to do the same

- Stick to your own role and responsibility and be adamant that you will not take on your partner's responsibilities too

- Begin observing your speech patterns. Avoid negative statements or negative suggestions

- Practice all this and stay alert to positive and negative signs–don't become complacent

- Set aside time for you both to discuss intimate issues that have been ignored or neglected.

I know it is very difficult to broach unwanted discussions in an intimate relationship. One or both of you may avoid certain issues. Remember that this is the reason you have reached this point where you are now. You have to take a deep breath and plunge in with what is troubling you. If the relationship is healthy and your partner wants to move forward with you, then your partner will respond in a sensitive, caring manner. If your partner becomes moody or angry, then s/he is not facing up to the difficulties, and not prepared to look at their part of the problem. In order to look at the truth of a situation, you both need to open up to each other, cross the pain barrier, and deal with the particular issue in question. If you cannot do this, how will your partnership improve? It will be devoid of passion. Here is an example:

A woman came to see me at the Counseling Surgery. She told me the tale of what happened when she'd found her husband reading pornographic magazines. She is a very attractive, interesting woman. They were sleeping apart because her husband said she snored and it was disturbing his sleep. One night after he had gone to bed, she was sleeping downstairs, when she sensed that the light was still on in his bedroom. She climbed the stairs, quietly, opened the bedroom door to find him masturbating to a pornographic magazine. She told me his face depicted lust and she was revolted by what she saw. She was no prude and would have happily looked at the magazine with him. But he had always told her that he didn't agree with pornography and the men who did read those magazines were perverts! She, of course, believed him.

She said nothing, turned on her heel and went down stairs. He followed her downstairs and was very angry at being 'caught out.' He projected his embarrassment (through anger) onto her and said, "Well, you have really opened up a can of worms this time." "Have I?" She replied. "Yes," he said, and "Please know I have to come clean and tell you that whilst I love you dearly you do nothing for me sexually." The sad man couldn't own up to wanting to see the magazines, instead, he projected his actions on to her so that she could take the responsibility for him. Blaming her was better for him than looking like a plonker. This is the action of a coward. Some considerable time later, she found him reading more pornographic magazines and when confronted again by her he took responsibility for his actions and told his wife that he had always enjoyed these magazines and assured her that it did not reflect on his feeling toward her. She had been worried that she was not enough for him sexually. This answer satisfied her fears.

Hidden Agendas

When we enter into a relationship, most of us are unaware of hidden agendas and mind games. In order to move on after betrayal, these hidden agendas and mind games need to be addressed. The two of you should own who you are, and with confidence express what you want from each other. Play it straight. Don't try to score over each other. Your relationship won't work that way. In order to move on from betrayal, you have to stay in awareness and trust your instinct.

What is a hidden agenda?

A hidden agenda is an underlying expectation of the relationship, or of your partner. A **reasonable** expectation can be discussed openly between you, whereas an **unreasonable** expectation cannot. You will have a very difficult time in a relationship when expectations are unreasonable, because our understanding of being unreasonable will differ. Here is an example:

Person A could be fastidiously clean and pristine both in their personal habits and at home and would expect others to be of similar mind, seeing this as a reasonable expectation. However, **Person B** could be of average tidiness and would seem like a slob to **Person A**. There would be immediate conflict between this partnership because neither have clearly identified what the word 'clean' means to each of them. The unconscious hidden agenda is 'you never reach my expectation of cleanliness'.

If you don't know what your partner's expectation is, how can you deliver? This scenario usually leads to disappointment by one or other partner. You only become disappointed if you expect too much. The trick is to not expect anyone else to do something that you wouldn't do yourself.

Hidden agendas are beneath the surface of all negotiations. This applies in business as well as emotional relationships. If these issues aren't unearthed, they will result in hostility and resentment. When you become employed as a Manager of an organization, one of the first tasks you undertake is a Strength, Weakness, Opportunity, and Threat (SWOT) analysis of the workplace. This is a good idea for emotional relationships also.

Strengths of the relationship

- You have financial security
- You love each other
- You have agreed goals
- You have identified and agreed 'roles and responsibilities'
- You both want to mend your relationship and 'move on'

Weaknesses in the relationship

- You do too much socializing
- You are spending too much money
- You are working too hard
- You have no quality time set aside to enjoy each other
- You have no agreed goals
- You have not identified 'roles and responsibilities'
- You have no financial security
- You don't know if you love each other

Opportunities to be explored

- The possibility of moving house
- The possibility of spending quality time with the children
- The possibility of planning exciting holidays for the family

- The possibility of new career opportunities
- The possibility of improving your career

Threats underlying the partnership

- My partner will leave me if I don't do as s/he says
- I am scared of my partner leaving me for someone else
- I am scared of being alone
- I am scared of having no money

The more communication there is between you, the less chance there is for unforeseen issues to arise.

What do you do when you unearth hidden agendas?

- Stop the discussion so that you both can think about the issue

- Try to understand the hidden agenda–explore all avenues

- Decide to discuss this issue at length and agree to be open and non-confrontational

- Decide for each of you to develop a plan to solve the issue after the discussion has taken place. Doing this separately will highlight the different opinions you hold regarding the subject, and you can both compromise on the issue

Often, when hidden agendas are discovered, the very act of discussing them enables both parties to find out how unreasonable/impractical they are. This is often enough to stop the process on that particular issue. Work as a team. Communicating in this way builds your confidence in the relationship. There is nothing more intimate than being able to say what you want to without it resulting in an argument. It is wonderful to know you are being heard and your opinions are valued and accepted by your partner. If you are able to do this it will bring you closer to each other. This will lead on to having the ultimate, loving, intimate, relationship. Trusting one another is vital. You have experienced bad times and the bubble you cocooned yourself in during the first flush of love has now well and truly burst by the betrayal you have experienced. You, or your partner, have fallen off the pedestal. However, you have both decided that you want the relationship to continue and are prepared to take the necessary steps to guarantee your future together.

Growing as a single unit

As well as growing and developing in the relationship, it is also important to grow independently. Don't feel guilty. Accept that you are a unique individual with needs that might be different to those of your partner. It is wrong to expect your partner to provide you with everything you want, wish, desire and need. Find out what you want to put into your life, e.g., retraining, courses, hobbies, friends, etc. Learn to value yourself and develop a personal program for your own advancement both professionally and socially. If you are living in a healthy relationship this should not cause any conflict between you. However, in an unhealthy relationship there will be problems. You will be made to feel guilty that you are leaving your partner out, moving on and not needing your partner to solve and provide everything for you anymore. This scenario can disable and demoralize your partner. Reassurances and support from you should be offered should this happen.

By now, both of you will have worked hard to re-establish yourselves as a partnership and, hopefully, learned and moved on from your bad experience. You should have begun to install a solid foundation to base your relationship on, and made bridges to compromise on issues that have been difficult to face and solve.

Where you are now

- You should have owned up to your part in the betrayal (when a betrayal occurs both partners are responsible in one way or another, as I have attempted to establish)

- You should have found how you contributed to the betrayal. If you have seen how you contributed to the betrayal then you have the power and understanding to improve this part of your relationship

- You should have taken the first step of introducing trust, loyalty, independence and confidence in your future together.

- You should have taken the first steps to being honest and independently self-aware and have joint awareness of your emotional, physical and financial circumstances

- You should be committed to the relationship

- There should be no fear of separation, divorce or abandonment

- There should be no fear of emotional outbursts and anger

- There should be no secrets and lies (only small inconsequential rubbish)

- You should both be able to manage your fear and anger

- You should have learned how to respond to each other during arguments

- You should respect each other and recognize the need for individual personal space

- You should share your feelings and not hold on to emotional worries

- You should trust one another

- You should recognize your limitations

- You should have forgiven your partner

- You should forgive yourself

- You should listen to your inner voice and take appropriate action.

- You should be able to trust your instinct and see things as they really are

- You should have stopped being fooled and coerced into doing something you don't want to do

- You should accept that this process you have experienced is an on-going strategy that you both should stick to.

Step 10 Acceptance and Forgiveness

> "To forgive is to overcome."
> Jeffrie G. Murphy, *Getting Even*

If you have forgiven an indiscretion by your partner, you should not raise the subject again. This, I believe, is an unwritten essential rule for the future success of your relationship. In 'moving on' after a betrayal there should be no recriminations. No looking back at problems. No re-living negative situations for any reason.

If you both believe that the relationship you have is worth keeping, then the betrayal must be put behind you, in order to achieve a deeper understanding and move forward together.

Remember you 'get back in life what you give out.' You must re-train and re-program your mind, your thoughts, your speech, and actions. In other words, brainwash yourself. Clear out old beliefs and be ready to put in better, more accurate beliefs. If you want to have a successful relationship, you must teach yourself to expect it.

Your inner dialogue is the key to future success.

Changing your negative inner dialogue into positive inner dialogue will have a magnetic effect on what life brings to you. Recognize that, in the past, you have negatively preconceived the outcome of certain situations. Maybe, you have manipulated the outcome. This outcome was reached as a result of all the experiences you have lived through in your life this far. Beliefs are inherited. You have been well schooled in believing that if you did *this*, then your partner would do *that*.

You may have seen this during your childhood, played out by your parents. You learned that you should 'give as good as you got.' You have been accustomed to retaliating indiscriminately and spontaneously. It only takes a few minutes to step out of the circle and see the situation through someone else's eyes. Be honest and try it.

Here are some examples of negative beliefs:

- Do you believe some people are luckier than others?
- Do you believe you are not meant to be happy?
- Do you believe you deserve what comes your way?
- Do you believe the world is against you?
- Do you believe that despite everything you do, nothing works out for you?
- Do you believe that you are trying hard and getting nowhere?
- Do you believe you were born to fail?

Which of the above statements you truly believe? Why do you believe it? Think hard and discover where the belief has come from, i.e., previous relationships, role models, friends, colleagues, parents, siblings. This exercise will help you to change your old fashioned or outdated belief systems.

> "If you wish to know the mind of a man,
> listen to his words." —Chinese Proverb

Here are some examples of positive beliefs:

- Do you believe you have what it takes to have a good life?
- Do you believe the phrase, "If it's meant to be, it's up to me?"

- Do you believe that "If you work hard you should play hard?"

- Do you believe that "Everything comes to those who wait?"

- Do you believe you have what it takes to be in a healthy relationship?

- Do you believe that your partner has what it takes to be in a healthy relationship with you?

From the moment of birth, you are trained (by your role models, siblings, teachers) to think and react in a particular way. This includes everything from expecting to be fed and watered, to surviving in difficult situations and emotional circumstances. Expectations are the views/beliefs you have of what you want from others. You project your beliefs/views on to those closest to you and are disappointed when they are unfulfilled. They for their part don't know what your expectations are, and neither do you on a conscious level. Take your mind back and think about how you have expected someone to react, only to discover that they reacted totally differently. Is it because you would have reacted in the way you expected that person to react? Were you projecting your reactions on to that person? This is the stuff disappointments are made of: **unrealistic beliefs and unrealistic expectations**. If you continue to use this model of negative thinking and expectation, you will be let down continually and become unmotivated and depressed.

To accept, forgive and move-on, you have to become the 'real' you. You must both be honest and reveal to each other who and what you are, and also what you want from your relationship. Accept that you cannot be the image of the person your partner has projected on to you and wants you to become. **You are 'You.'** You should not allow anyone to mold you into becoming a different person from who you are. No-one else should control who you are. Only you are responsible for how you react, the thoughts you have, the things you say and do. When we are' in love' we are blissfully ignorant of hidden agendas and projected fantasy images that permeate through the very foundation of our relationship.

It's only when you have a crisis in your relationship that all these underlying issues come to the forefront. Ask yourself, "Has the relationship come to this point because we both failed our quest to become the person each of us has projected on to the other?" Your relationship has to be real, only real relationships move on and enjoy the ultimate intimacy that an honest partnership enjoys.

It is courageous to be who you really are:

- Will you be liked?
- Will you be loved?
- Will you be accepted by family and friends and work colleagues?

To be the real you is a challenge. Be brave, and do it.

> "And above all, have fervent love for one another: for love shall cover the multitude of sins."
>
> —Peter 4.8

> "We need people in our lives with whom we can be as open as possible. To have real conversation with people may seem like such a simple, obvious suggestion, but it involves courage and risk."
>
> —Thomas Moore

Emotional Acceptance

You have emotionally accepted someone and yourself, when you can confirm some or all of the following:

- I accept that I cannot change my partner
- I accept that I can only change me
- I accept that I was responsible, in part, for the betrayal
- I accept that the relationship was not based on honesty
- I accept that my expectations of my partner were unrealistic
- I accept that my partner's expectations of me were unrealistic
- I accept the lack of communication that existed in the relationship
- I accept that we had both stopped making an effort for each other
- I accept we were both in a 'comfortable' rut [may have only been true of one.]
- I accept that my focus had shifted from the relationship
- I accept that there was no trust in the relationship.

The list is endless. Make your own list. You will be surprised at what you will discover about yourself, and your part in the relationship.

A strategy for your future:

- To communicate at a deeper level
- To be honest with each other
- To avoid criticism and blame
- To be understanding and compassionate

- To detach from problems in order to see them objectively instead of emotionally
- To build on the positive aspects in the relationship
- To compromise on the negative aspects of the relationship
- To understand that there is a positive and negative interpretation of every situation
- Not to expect my partner to provide all that I need
- To trust each other.

It is impossible to stick to a strategy all of the time. However, it is a good yardstick to measure how far you have come in a relationship, and to purposefully read the strategy (or pledge) on a regular basis. This will prompt you both to the agreement you have jointly made regarding your future together.

The strategy can act as a 'way forward' agreement made by the two of you in order to identify that you are committed to the continuation of the relationship.

What happens if one of you slips up and starts repeating old patterns?

It is essential for you both to agree that, if one of you slips back into rejected old patterns and habits, (people *always* have temporary slips back into rejected old habits) then the other partner can and must point this out to stop you both slipping back even further. Once reminded of the changes that you jointly decided upon, you will be able to, quickly, address the issue. If these slip-ups are caught early enough, they will be only temporary blips. Otherwise, they are the start of a slide back into the old pattern. It is good to have this understanding with your partner, as a prompt from either of you can prevent the spiral down to the old repeating patterns of behavior.

Should neither partner spot the slip-up at the time it happens, a conflict will occur. When this happens you will both know that something you have said or done was wrong. Do not apportion blame on either of you. Accept that it has happened and swiftly 'move on'.

Forgive yourselves for the mistakes you will undoubtedly make. You cannot and will not always get it right.

I hope that, in this book, you have found the necessary emotional tools to assist you in the 'moving on' process after a betrayal has occurred. I wish to 'good luck' for your future together.

> "You must speak straight so that your words may go as sunlight to our hearts."   —Cochise

"A Second Chance"

I though it would kill me
I wanted to die.
The dreams of our future
Were gone from my mind

Were my eyes shut?
Did I ignore the signs?
The life we both lived
Has been horribly maligned

I search for the truth
I open my eyes
To see with clarity
To understand why

A second chance is offered
The door is open wide
Shall I walk through it?
Will I survive?

Am I just weak?
Or am I strong?
Do I stay in this relationship
Even though I was wronged?

It takes two in a partnership
Both striving for success
We will both try again
For our future happiness!

Lynda Bevan

About the Author

Lynda Bevan lives in a picturesque village in South Wales, United Kingdom. She is 59 years of age, married for the third time, with three (adult) children. During her teens and early twenties she pursued and enjoyed acting and taught drama at local Youth Centers.

Her 22 year career has involved working in the area of mental health, with the two major care agencies in the UK, Social Services and the National Health Service.

After the birth of her third child, and with her second marriage ending, she became employed by Social Services and climbed through the ranks to senior management level with some speed.

During her career with Social Services she developed a passion for counseling and psychotherapy and worked extensively with mental health patients within the organization, setting up counseling projects in Healthcare Centers. The task was to tackle the issue of doctors who inappropriately referred patients to Psychiatric Hospitals for therapy when they had experienced events that arise in normal everyday life, e.g., divorce, anxiety, depression, bereavement, stress, loss of role. It was during this time that she became involved in marital/relationship counseling and, coincidentally, was experiencing difficulties within her own relationship. The experience of working in this environment, and her own relationship issues, enabled Lynda to be innovative; creating methods of coping and developing strategies that enabled her and her patients to live within their problematic relationships. These strategies were devised and offered to patients who had clearly identified that they did not want to separate or proceed with the divorce process.

After taking early retirement from Social Services, she became employed by the National Health Service as a Counselor in the Primary Healthcare Setting. During this period in her career, she began using the strategies she had developed with patients who were referred for relationship counseling and who did not want to end their partnership/marriage. These strategies have been used extensively over a ten year period with impressive results.

Lynda is presently employed as a Manager of a charity that supports people who are HIV positive. She is also the Resident Relationship Counselor on Swansea Sound Radio.

Index

Life After Your Lover Walks Out
Book #1 in the 10-Step Empowerment Series

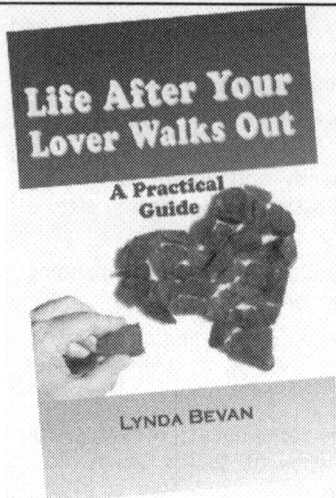

Your long-time partner has just walked out on you forever:

- Do you feel paralyzed or afraid to move on?
- Does the thought or sight of your old partner with someone else fill you with rage?
- Are you worried or anxious about how to get by financially on your own?
- Are you afraid to start another relationship with a new partner?
- Do you lack energy and motivation to do anything at all since the break-up?
- Do you spend a lot of time thinking how it might have been different?

If you answered **yes** to any of these, this book is for you!

Praise *for Life After Your Lover Walks Out*

"This is a well thought out, useful little book that is an excellent guide for those recovering form a broken, long-term relationship."
-Robert Rich, PhD, M.A.P.S., author of Cancer: A Personal Challenge

"An excellent tool to help persons move on after the end of a relationship. *Life After Your Lover Walks Out* highlights the common cognitive distortions and exaggerated emotions and urges the reader to examine their actions and how they perpetuate their feeling of loss. Through the use of introspective questions the book invites the reader to take a journey of self examination in order to accept the loss and to reengage in life." -Ian Landry, MA, MSW, Case Manager

Loving Healing Press
5145 Pontiac Trail
Ann Arbor, MI 48105
(734)662-6864
info@LovingHealing.com
Dist. Baker & Taylor

Pub. July 2006
trade/paper — 6"x9"
ISBN-13 978-1-932690-26-2
$14.95 Retail
Includes bibliography, resources, and index.
For general libraries.